Unveiling the Truth & Breaking the Chains:

Divine 9 Greek Letters and God's Word

Apostle Latina C. Campbell

Print ISBN: 978-1-955312-78-3
eBook ISBN: 978-1-955312-79-0

Printed in the United States of America

Story Corner Publishing & Consulting, Inc.
Chesapeake, VA 23325

Storycornerpublishing@yahoo.com

www.StoryCornerPublishing.com

Dedication

I dedicate this book to all that want to be a part of something bigger than they are and give back to those in need. There are many ways to go about it. So, widen your perspective and allow God to lead you into the unknown.

Table of Contents

Introduction

Testimonial: My Journey Through Zeta Phi Beta and Into the Light of God

In the spring of 2013, a Zeta was born, and "Express Delivery" was formed. I was #3 and my line name was "Blue Apparition," meaning ghost. They named me this because in the beginning I was a single mother who had to work two jobs to make ends meet, so I could not be a part of every meeting or event. Therefore, I was considered "missing in action" or a ghost to them. I was honored they still considered me and could not believe I made the cut. I finally fulfilled a childhood dream—I became a member of Zeta Phi Beta Sorority, Incorporated (Grad Chapter- Gamma Nu Zeta) in Camden, NJ.

Growing up in an inner-city environment plagued by challenges such as drugs, gang violence, poverty, and prostitution, I always wanted to make a difference in my community. Organizations like Zeta Phi Beta seemed to be the perfect avenue for change, offering opportunities to serve, uplift, and bring hope to those in need.

Becoming a Zeta was everything I had hoped for—or so I thought. The excitement of joining an organization with a rich legacy of service and sisterhood filled me with pride. We hosted community initiatives, parties, fundraisers, and networking events. From the outside, it looked like I was thriving, but deep inside, I felt an unshakable emptiness. I didn't understand what was missing.

No matter how many good deeds I participated in or how much joy I brought to others, I couldn't shake the feeling of a void in my life. I thought my work in the sorority would bring me fulfillment, but my life began to spiral further out of control. I kept searching for something that could give me the peace and purpose I desperately needed.

In August of 2016, I hit rock bottom. It was during that dark period that God revealed Himself to me in an unforgettable way. One night while working a midnight shift at the Liberty Bell in Philadelphia, Pennsylvania, I felt God's presence. God spoke to me clearly, telling me it was time to surrender to Him or risk losing my life to the world. At that moment, I knew the world could not offer me anything. I had to live—not just for myself, but for my two children.

Standing before the Liberty Bell, I realized the profound significance of liberty which was freedom. I had the choice to be free and it was there in that moment I was set free. I opened my heart to God, accepting Him as my Lord and Savior, my guide, protector, and provider. From that day forward, my life began to change.

I started immersing myself in prayer, studying the Bible, fasting, and allowing God to lead me in cutting toxic relationships, habits, and attachments from my life. The clarity and peace that followed were unlike anything I had ever experienced. For the first time, I understood why my life had felt so chaotic and unfulfilled—my foundation had been built on things that were not rooted in God.

It was during this transformative time that God led me to give up many things, including my dream of joining a motorcycle club. I was prepared to walk away from that, but when God instructed me to leave Zeta Phi Beta Sorority, I hesitated. After all, we were doing so much good in the community—how could that be wrong?

God began to show me the spiritual roots of the sorority, revealing that it was not founded on Him. While many of its activities seemed good on the surface, I learned that not all "good" things are of God. Just because something appears positive doesn't mean it aligns with His will. The Bible warns us about Satan's deception and how he can use seemingly harmless things to lead us astray.

Walking away from the sorority was one of the hardest decisions I've ever made, but it was also one of the most necessary. I realized that I didn't need to be part of an organization to give back or to help my community—I could do so in ways that fully honored God.

As I obeyed God and left the sorority behind, He began to elevate me in ways I could have never imagined. He called me to start my own ministry and eventually to the office and role of an Apostle, serving His people alongside my husband and children. Today, I am honored to help others open their hearts to God and experience His love, grace, and transformative power. I remember leading other women and even young girls to Zeta. Now I lead others to Jesus Christ/Yeshua.

Looking back, I have no regrets about leaving Zeta Phi Beta Sorority. While I cherish the lessons learned and the people I met, I know that God had a greater plan for me. I pray for all those drawn to Greek-letter organizations, that they may come to understand the truth and be set free from the spiritual chains that often go unseen.

God's grace, mercy, and love saved my life. He gave me a new purpose and a new foundation, built solely on Him. Now, I live every day to show my love for Him through obedience and action. My prayer is that my testimony will inspire others to seek the truth, trust in God's plan, and experience the freedom only He can give.

Purpose of the Book

The Divine Nine organizations—Alpha Phi Alpha, Alpha Kappa Alpha, Kappa Alpha Psi, Omega Psi Phi, Delta Sigma Theta, Phi Beta Sigma, **Zeta Phi Beta**, Sigma Gamma Rho, and Iota Phi Theta—are well-regarded for their historical impact, community service, and promotion of academic excellence as well as other Greek Organizations. These organizations have been pillars of strength in the Black community, uplifting countless individuals and providing networks of support. However, for Believers of Jesus/ Yeshua, membership in these organizations can pose questions about the compatibility of their practices and principles with biblical teachings.

This book is not written to vilify the Divine Nine or to dismiss their contributions to society. Rather, its purpose is to encourage members and potential members who profess faith in Jesus Christ/Yeshua to critically examine these organizations through the lens of scripture. It is a call to discernment, seeking to understand how our affiliations align—or conflict—with the Word of God.

A Personal Journey

For many Believers, joining a Divine Nine organization is a deeply personal decision. It may stem from family traditions, a desire for social connection, or the opportunity to contribute to meaningful causes. Yet, as followers of Christ, every decision— including the organizations we join—must be weighed against our primary allegiance to God.

This book arises from the experiences of countless believers, including myself, who have wrestled with reconciling their faith with the practices, oaths, and symbols of these organizations. Some have found peace in remaining active members, while others have chosen to separate themselves after deeper reflection on scripture. Wherever you find yourself, this book seeks to provide guidance rooted in biblical truth.

Why Examine the Divine Nine?

1. Cultural vs. Spiritual Priorities

Black Greek-letter organizations have been a source of pride and empowerment, especially in the face of systemic racism and marginalization. They provide community, mentorship, and a sense of belonging. However, as Believers of Christ, we are called to ensure that our cultural identities and affiliations do not overshadow our spiritual identity in Christ (Galatians 3:28).

2. Rituals and Symbols

Many Divine Nine rituals incorporate elements that raise spiritual concerns for Believers. From secret oaths to symbolic gestures, these practices often draw from sources that may conflict with biblical teachings. Are these elements simply cultural expressions, or do they carry deeper spiritual implications?

3. Allegiance and Worship

The Bible is clear: our ultimate allegiance belongs to God alone (Exodus 20:3). This raises questions about the nature of fraternity and sorority commitments. Can Believers of Christ fully commit to these organizations without compromising their devotion to Christ?

4. **A Call to Discernment**

Philippians 1:9-10 encourages believers to "abound in knowledge and depth of insight, so that you may be able to discern what is best and may be pure and blameless for the day of Christ." This book invites readers to apply this biblical principle, examining their affiliations with prayer, wisdom, and a heart fully devoted to God.

The Approach of This Book

This book is written with respect for the Divine Nine and their legacy. It is not an attack but an invitation to consider how faith and membership intersect. It seeks to:

- Provide a biblical framework for evaluating the practices and principles of these organizations.

- Present testimonies of those who have navigated the challenges of balancing faith with fraternity/sorority life.

- Equip readers with spiritual tools for making informed, God-honoring decisions.

Who This Book Is For

- Believers of Christ currently involved in Divine Nine organizations who are seeking guidance on how to reconcile their faith with their membership.

- Potential members who want to understand the spiritual implications of joining.

- Church leaders, pastors, and family members who want to support loved ones navigating this journey.

A Journey Toward Truth

Ultimately, this book is about more than the Divine Nine. It is about living a life fully surrendered to Christ, in every area, including our affiliations. By examining these organizations through the lens of scripture, we can grow in our understanding of God's will and ensure that our lives reflect His glory.

As you read, I encourage you to approach this topic with an open heart, a commitment to scripture, and a desire to honor God above all else. The journey may be challenging, but it is one worth taking for the sake of your faith and spiritual integrity.

Chapter 1:

The History of the Divine Nine

Origins and Purpose

The Divine Nine, formally known as the National Pan-Hellenic Council (NPHC), consists of nine historically Black Greek-letter organizations (BGLOs) that were established to promote unity, scholarship, and community uplift among African Americans. These organizations emerged during a time of systemic racism, exclusion, and segregation, where Black students were often denied access to opportunities afforded to their white counterparts.

The first of these organizations, Alpha Phi Alpha Fraternity, was founded in 1906 at Cornell University as a brotherhood focused on academic excellence and service. Soon after, others followed, including Alpha Kappa Alpha Sorority (1908), Kappa Alpha Psi Fraternity (1911), and Delta Sigma Theta Sorority (1913). Each organization was born out of the need to create a safe space for African American students to foster leadership, academic achievement, and mutual support.

These organizations have been instrumental in breaking racial barriers, advancing civil rights, and serving their communities. Members of the Divine Nine include many notable figures such as Dr. Martin Luther King Jr. (Alpha Phi Alpha), Rosa Parks (Alpha Kappa Alpha), and Shirley Chisholm (Delta Sigma Theta), who used their platforms to enact social change.

Core Mission and Values

At their core, Divine Nine organizations emphasize:

1. **Scholarship**: Encouraging academic excellence and lifelong learning.

2. **Leadership**: Cultivating leaders who advocate for justice and equality.

3. **Service**: Commitment to community uplift through philanthropy and volunteerism.

4. **Unity**: Building strong bonds of brotherhood and sisterhood among members.

These values resonate deeply within the Black community, particularly as they address systemic inequities and provide mentorship to younger generations. However, while these goals are noble, Christians must consider how these organizations' practices align with their faith.

Structure and Practices

Each organization in the Divine Nine operates under a Greek-letter system, inspired by the fraternity and sorority models found in predominantly white institutions. Members adopt unique symbols, colors, mottos, and rituals that reflect their organization's identity and purpose.

Key Practices Include:

1. **Rituals and Initiations**: These are designed to bond members and instill loyalty to the organization. Many

rituals are secretive, involving oaths and symbolic acts that are central to the fraternity or sorority experience.

2. **Public Displays of Unity**: This includes step shows, strolls, and calls—expressions of pride and camaraderie.

3. **Service Projects**: Members participate in community service activities as part of their organizational mission.

4. **Networking and Brotherhood/Sisterhood**: Members build lifelong connections that extend beyond college life.

Spiritual Implications of the Divine Nine's History

From a cultural and historical perspective, the Divine Nine's emergence is a testament to the resilience and ingenuity of the Black community. These organizations have filled gaps left by systemic racism, offering opportunities for empowerment and progress. However, the influence of Greek culture, secretive rituals, and the elevation of organizational loyalty can raise questions for Christians regarding their spiritual significance.

Biblical Considerations:

1. The Use of Greek Symbols and Mythology:

The adoption of Greek letters and symbols often ties these organizations to aspects of Greek mythology. While these may be used symbolically or as part of tradition, Christians must ask whether such associations align with their faith in the God of the Bible. Exodus 20:4-5 warns against creating or revering symbols that may detract from worship of the one true God.

2. **The Concept of Brotherhood and Sisterhood**:

While brotherhood and sisterhood are foundational to the Divine Nine, the Bible emphasizes spiritual family as paramount (Matthew 12:48-50). Christians are called to prioritize their relationship with fellow believers in Christ over earthly affiliations.

3. **Oaths and Allegiances**:

Many Divine Nine organizations require members to take oaths during initiation. Scripture, however, cautions against making binding vows that conflict with allegiance to God (Matthew 5:34-37). I remember taking this very oath, singing this hymn, and chanting this chant. I believed every word and was proud of it.

Zeta Phi Beta Oath

I hereby pledge myself to be loyal to every rule and regulation of Zeta Phi Beta Sorority. I will conduct myself at all times in such a manner as will not bring reproach upon my sisters. Should I be guilty of wrong-doing, I will willingly accept any corrections given to me by my sisters. I will strive at all times to exhibit the highest levels of culture, to put forth zeal for those things which stand for righteousness and hold within my heart a love which will unite us as one. God grant that I may ever have the spirit of democracy for all my fellowmen and keep this Oath before me daily.

Z Phi B hymn

Verse 1: With fervent hearts we pray For you Zeta each day You've always stood for the right, Rather than for the might We will love you ever And forsake you never When Zeta calls, we'll answer one and all Chorus: Zeta Phi Beta, we love you so! Your very name sets our hearts aglow You're brave and you will see That Zeta Phi Beta means victory!

Zeta's Chant

Every beat of my heart is crying Z Phi B

The Social and Cultural Legacy

The Divine Nine have undeniably contributed to the betterment of society. They have:

- Championed civil rights and voter advocacy initiatives.

- Established scholarships and mentorship programs for underserved youth.

- Fostered a sense of pride and unity within the Black community.

However, for Christians, the question remains: Does participation in these organizations require compromises that could conflict with their faith? Can one fully uphold their biblical convictions while engaging in the practices and rituals of these fraternities and sororities?

The history of the Divine Nine is one of resilience, empowerment, and progress. They have played a vital role in shaping the Black experience in America, creating opportunities and addressing systemic inequities. However, as Christians, we are called to evaluate every aspect of our lives—including cultural affiliations—through the lens of scripture. While honoring the Divine Nine's legacy, we must also critically assess whether their practices align with God's Word.

Chapter 2:

Biblical Teachings on Allegiance and Worship

The Bible is clear that our primary allegiance is to God. As Christians, we are called to worship Him in spirit and truth, placing no other entity, person, or organization above Him. In this chapter, we will explore biblical teachings on allegiance, worship, and community, and how these principles apply to our daily lives, including the affiliations we choose.

1. Allegiance to God Alone

Key Scriptures:

- *"You shall have no other gods before me."* (Exodus 20:3)

- *"No one can serve two masters. Either you will hate the one and love the other, or you will be devoted to the one and despise the other."* (Matthew 6:24)

The Bible repeatedly emphasizes that God demands exclusive devotion from His people. Allegiance to Him means prioritizing His will and commandments over any earthly commitments.

Application to Modern Affiliations:

- Joining an organization often involves pledging loyalty, which can sometimes conflict with the Christian's ultimate loyalty to God. For example, if the values or practices of an organization contradict biblical principles, Christians must choose to honor God over the group.

• In Divine Nine organizations, members take oaths during initiation ceremonies. These oaths, while intended to foster unity and commitment, must be carefully examined to ensure they do not require allegiance that supersedes one's devotion to Christ.

2. Idolatry: More Than Just Statues

Key Scriptures:

• *"Dear children, keep yourselves from idols."* (1 John 5:21)

• *"You shall not make for yourself an image in the form of anything in heaven above or on the earth beneath or in the waters below. You shall not bow down to them or worship them."* (Exodus 20:4-5)

Idolatry in the Bible is not limited to worshiping carved images or false gods. It extends to anything that takes the place of God in our lives—whether it's an organization, a symbol, or an activity.

Examples of Modern Idolatry:

• Placing loyalty to a group, organization, or ideology above God.

• Revering symbols, rituals, or traditions in ways that detract from the worship of God.

• Allowing participation in an organization to overshadow Christian responsibilities, such as evangelism or personal holiness.

Divine Nine Concerns:

• Many Divine Nine organizations use specific symbols, chants, and rituals to foster identity and pride among members. While these may seem harmless, Christians must discern whether such practices conflict with biblical teachings on idolatry.

• For instance, do members place excessive value on their organization's symbols or traditions, elevating them to a level of reverence that borders on idolatry?

3. Worship: Spirit and Truth

Key Scripture:

• *"Yet a time is coming and has now come when the true worshipers will worship the Father in the Spirit and in truth, for they are the kind of worshipers the Father seeks."* (John 4:23)

Worship is more than singing hymns or attending church services; it is a lifestyle of devotion to God. True worship requires aligning our actions, thoughts, and commitments with His Word.

The Nature of Worship:

• Worship involves acknowledging God as the supreme authority in every aspect of life.

- It includes rejecting practices or allegiances that contradict His Word.

Potential Conflicts:

- Some initiation rites or ceremonies within the Divine Nine may include elements that resemble acts of worship, such as kneeling, chanting, or performing symbolic acts. While these actions are often symbolic and intended to honor the organization, Christians must ask: Do these practices detract from their worship of God?

4. Making Oaths and Vows

Key Scriptures:

- *"But I tell you, do not swear an oath at all: either by heaven, for it is God's throne; or by the earth, for it is his footstool."* (Matthew 5:34-35)

- *"It is better not to make a vow than to make one and not fulfill it."* (Ecclesiastes 5:5)

Oaths are serious commitments. In biblical times, they were made to God alone and often carried significant consequences if broken. Jesus Himself warned against making unnecessary oaths, encouraging His followers instead to let their "yes" be yes and their "no" be no.

Concerns with Divine Nine Oaths:

- Many Divine Nine organizations require members to take oaths during initiation. These oaths often include pledges of loyalty and secrecy.

- Christians must critically evaluate whether such oaths conflict with their ultimate commitment to God. Does the oath bind them to values or practices that contradict scripture?

5. Community and Brotherhood/Sisterhood

Key Scriptures:

- *"For whoever does the will of my Father in heaven is my brother and sister and mother."* (Matthew 12:50)

- *"Do not be yoked together with unbelievers. For what do righteousness and wickedness have in common?"* (2 Corinthians 6:14)

The Bible highlights the importance of community among believers, emphasizing spiritual unity over earthly affiliations. While earthly relationships, such as brotherhood and sisterhood, are valuable, they must never take precedence over one's spiritual family in Christ.

The Christian Perspective on Brotherhood/Sisterhood:

- The Divine Nine promotes strong bonds among members, often describing these relationships as lifelong and unbreakable. While this can foster unity, Christians must ensure that their primary allegiance is to their spiritual family.

- Additionally, Christians should consider whether their organization's values align with biblical teachings on community and righteousness.

The Bible offers clear guidance on allegiance, worship, and community. As Christians, we are called to:

1. Serve God with undivided devotion.

2. Reject idolatry in all forms, including excessive reverence for symbols, rituals, or organizations.

3. Be cautious about taking oaths or making commitments that conflict with our faith.

4. Prioritize our spiritual family and live in alignment with God's Word.

Chapter 3:

Analyzing Divine Nine Practices

The Divine Nine organizations are rich in tradition, with rituals, symbols, and practices that foster a sense of unity, pride, and identity among their members. These practices are often central to the fraternity or sorority experience, helping to establish a deep bond between members and their organization. However, for Christians, it is crucial to evaluate these practices in light of biblical teachings. This chapter explores some of the key elements of Divine Nine organizations—rituals, symbols, and oaths—and their potential spiritual implications.

1. Rituals and Initiations

One of the hallmarks of Divine Nine organizations is their initiation process, which often includes secret rituals. These rituals are designed to create a sense of exclusivity, loyalty, and belonging. While these practices may seem harmless on the surface, Christians must consider their spiritual implications.

Common Features of Divine Nine Rituals:

• **Secrecy**: Initiation rituals are typically kept confidential, with members sworn to secrecy about their content.

• **Symbolic Acts**: These may include kneeling, chanting, or symbolic gestures.

• **Oaths and Pledges**: Members often recite vows of loyalty to the organization and its ideals.

- **Cultural or Spiritual Overtones**: Some rituals draw on elements of Greek mythology, African spirituality, or other non-Christian influences.

Biblical Concerns with Rituals:

1. **Secrecy**: The Bible warns against secrecy when it comes to spiritual matters. Jesus said, *"For there is nothing hidden that will not be disclosed, and nothing concealed that will not be known or brought out into the open"* (Luke 8:17). Christians are called to walk in the light, and practices shrouded in secrecy can raise questions about their alignment with biblical values.

2. **Symbolic Acts of Worship**: Rituals that involve kneeling, chanting, or other acts can resemble worship. Exodus 20:5 warns against bowing down to anything other than God.

3. **Oaths**: As discussed in Chapter 2, taking oaths that bind one's loyalty to anything other than God can conflict with biblical teachings (Matthew 5:34-37).

Questions for Reflection:

- Do these rituals align with my faith in Christ?

- Do they glorify God or elevate the organization above Him?

- Would I be comfortable sharing these rituals with my pastor or Christian community?

2. Symbols and Iconography

Each Divine Nine organization has unique symbols, colors, and emblems that represent its identity and values. While these elements are often used to inspire pride and unity, they can carry deeper spiritual implications.

Examples of Common Symbols:

- Animals (e.g., owls, doves, dogs, elephants) associated with specific organizations.

- Letters from the Greek alphabet.

- Shields, crests, and mottos.

- Colors representing the organization's identity.

Biblical Concerns with Symbols:

1. **Symbolism in Worship**: The Bible warns against creating or revering symbols that detract from God's glory. Exodus 20:4-5 prohibits the making and worshiping of graven images. While members may not explicitly worship these symbols, the level of reverence shown toward them can sometimes approach idolatry.

2. **Greek Mythology**: Many symbols and letters used by Divine Nine organizations are rooted in Greek culture and mythology, which often involves deities and practices that conflict with Christian teachings. Christians must consider whether adopting these symbols is compatible with their faith.

Reflection Questions:

- Do I place undue importance on these symbols?

- Do they hold spiritual significance that conflicts with my belief in the one true God?

- Can I glorify God while using these symbols?

3. Oaths and Pledges

The pledging process in Divine Nine organizations typically involves reciting oaths or vows of loyalty. These pledges are often made during initiation ceremonies and are considered binding commitments to the organization and its values.

Biblical Perspective on Oaths:

1. **Making Vows**: Ecclesiastes 5:4-5 says, *"When you make a vow to God, do not delay to fulfill it. He has no pleasure in fools; fulfill your vow. It is better not to make a vow than to make one and not fulfill it."* Oaths and vows are serious matters in the Bible, and Christians are cautioned against making unnecessary or conflicting commitments.

2. **Divided Loyalty**: Pledging loyalty to an organization can sometimes lead to divided allegiance, especially if the organization's values or practices conflict with biblical teachings. Matthew 6:24 warns that no one can serve two masters.

Questions for Reflection:

- Does this oath conflict with my commitment to Christ?

- Am I pledging allegiance to ideals or practices that contradict biblical principles?

- Would I be willing to renounce this oath if it conflicted with my faith?

4. Brotherhood, Sisterhood, and Exclusivity

One of the strongest appeals of Divine Nine organizations is the sense of brotherhood or sisterhood they provide. Members often describe their organizations as lifelong families, offering support and connection that extend beyond college.

Biblical Perspective on Community:

1. **Christian Fellowship**: The Bible emphasizes the importance of spiritual family. Jesus said, *"Whoever does God's will is my brother and sister and mother"* (Mark 3:35). While earthly relationships are valuable, Christians are called to prioritize their spiritual family in Christ.

2. **Exclusivity**: Some Divine Nine organizations emphasize exclusivity, where membership grants special privileges or status. James 2:1 warns against favoritism, reminding believers that all are equal in Christ.

Questions for Reflection:

- Does my membership in this organization hinder my ability to prioritize my spiritual family?

- Am I upholding biblical principles of love, humility, and equality in my interactions with non-members?

5. Potential Conflicts with Christian Witness

Membership in Divine Nine organizations can sometimes lead to situations where Christians must compromise their values. This might include:

• Participating in events or traditions that conflict with Christian beliefs.

• Feeling pressured to prioritize organizational loyalty over spiritual commitments.

• Facing challenges in sharing the gospel due to perceived conflicts between faith and fraternity/sorority life.

Reflection Questions:

• Does my membership enhance or hinder my ability to share Christ with others?

• Am I honoring God in every aspect of my involvement?

• Do I feel convicted about any part of my participation in this organization?

Rituals, symbols, and oaths are central to the Divine Nine experience, but Christians must carefully evaluate these practices in light of biblical teachings. While these elements may foster unity and pride, they can also pose spiritual challenges for believers seeking to live in full obedience to Christ.

Chapter 4:

Biblical Concerns with Specific Elements of the Divine Nine

While Divine Nine organizations emphasize service, leadership, and community uplift, certain elements within their traditions and practices warrant closer scrutiny from a biblical perspective. This chapter focuses on identifying specific areas of concern, examining their potential conflicts with Christian principles, and offering a balanced analysis to guide believers in their discernment.

1. Oaths of Secrecy and Allegiance

What They Are:
During initiation, members often take oaths of secrecy and loyalty. These vows are intended to solidify commitment to the organization and its members, ensuring confidentiality regarding rituals and internal affairs.

Biblical Analysis:

- **Prohibition of Unnecessary Oaths**:

Jesus instructed His followers, *"Do not swear an oath at all... Let your 'Yes' be 'Yes,' and your 'No,' 'No'"* (Matthew 5:34-37). This teaching encourages honesty without the need for elaborate promises, especially those that could bind someone to conflicting loyalties.

- **Allegiance to God Alone**:

The first commandment states, *"You shall have no other gods before me"* (Exodus 20:3). Oaths that require unwavering allegiance to an organization could inadvertently rival one's devotion to God.

Concerns for Christians:

- Does the oath require absolute loyalty to the organization, placing it above or equal to one's commitment to God?

- Could the secrecy involved in these oaths lead to actions or commitments that are spiritually compromising?

Reflection:

Christians should carefully evaluate whether taking such oaths aligns with their biblical commitment to truth, transparency, and undivided allegiance to God.

2. Symbolism and Iconography

What They Are:

The Divine Nine organizations use symbols, crests, and colors to represent their identity and values. Many of these symbols are derived from Greek mythology or historical references, such as animals, letters, or other cultural motifs.

Biblical Analysis:

- **Warnings Against Idolatry**:

The Bible cautions against revering objects or symbols in ways that might detract from God's glory. *"You shall not make for yourself an image... You shall not bow down to them or worship them"* (Exodus 20:4-5).

- **Roots in Greek Mythology**:

Some organizations incorporate elements tied to Greek gods and myths. While often symbolic, Christians must discern whether such associations conflict with their worship of the one true God.

Concerns for Christians:

- Do these symbols hold spiritual or cultural significance that contradicts biblical teachings?

- Does the reverence given to these symbols resemble acts of idolatry or detract from one's devotion to God?

Reflection:
Christians should ask themselves whether their participation in the use or reverence of these symbols aligns with their call to glorify God alone.

3. Ritual Practices

What They Are:
Initiation and membership rituals are central to Divine Nine organizations. These often involve symbolic acts, chanting, and sometimes physical demonstrations of commitment.

Biblical Analysis:

- **Acts of Worship**:

Rituals that resemble acts of worship—such as kneeling, chanting, or symbolic gestures—should be examined in light of

"Worship the Lord your God, and serve Him only" (Matthew 4:10).

- **Pagan Influences**:

Some rituals incorporate elements from cultural or spiritual traditions outside of Christianity. Colossians 2:8 warns, *"See to it that no one takes you captive through hollow and deceptive philosophy, which depends on human tradition and the elemental spiritual forces of this world rather than on Christ."*

Concerns for Christians:

- Are the rituals reflective of values that conflict with Christian teachings?

- Do the rituals require participation in symbolic acts that could be construed as spiritual in nature?

Reflection:
Participation in rituals should be evaluated carefully to ensure that they do not lead to compromises in one's faith or inadvertently engage in practices contrary to God's Word.

4. Brotherhood, Sisterhood, and Exclusivity

What It Is:
The Divine Nine emphasizes strong bonds of brotherhood and sisterhood, often describing these relationships as lifelong and exclusive. Members often prioritize these connections above others, fostering a sense of pride and loyalty.

Biblical Analysis:

- **The Priority of Spiritual Family**:

Jesus redefined family in spiritual terms, saying, *"Whoever does the will of my Father in heaven is my brother and sister and mother"* (Matthew 12:50). While earthly relationships are valuable, they should not supersede one's spiritual family in Christ.

- **Favoritism and Exclusivity**:

James 2:1 warns against favoritism, urging Christians to treat all people equally as image-bearers of God.

Concerns for Christians:

- Does membership in the Divine Nine encourage exclusivity that contradicts the inclusivity of the gospel?

- Do the bonds of brotherhood or sisterhood overshadow relationships within the body of Christ?

Reflection:
Christians must ensure that their sense of belonging and identity is rooted primarily in Christ and His church, rather than in an earthly organization.

5. Service and Community Involvement

What It Is:
A cornerstone of Divine Nine organizations is their commitment to community service and philanthropy. Members often participate in activities that uplift the Black community, promote education, and advocate for social justice.

Biblical Analysis:

- ### Alignment with God's Call to Serve:

The Bible calls Christians to serve others. *"Whatever you did for one of the least of these brothers and sisters of mine, you did for me"* (Matthew 25:40). Acts of service and advocacy align with biblical values when done with the right heart and purpose.

- ### Motivations for Service:

Scripture emphasizes serving for God's glory rather than human recognition (Colossians 3:23-24).

Concerns for Christians:

- Are acts of service motivated by genuine love for others and a desire to glorify God?

- Does membership in the Divine Nine lead to serving in ways that overshadow one's call to serve within the church?

Reflection:
While the service aspect of the Divine Nine is commendable, Christians must ensure that their ultimate motivation and purpose align with glorifying God rather than elevating the organization.

The practices of the Divine Nine organizations—oaths, symbols, rituals, and community bonds—present opportunities for both service and spiritual challenges. While many of these elements may appear neutral or even positive, they must be critically examined in light of biblical teachings.

Chapter 5:

A Call to Spiritual Discernment

The ability to discern truth from deception is a vital skill for any believer. Spiritual discernment, rooted in wisdom and guided by the Holy Spirit, equips Christians to navigate the complexities of life while remaining faithful to God. In this chapter, we delve deeper into the necessity of spiritual discernment, the dangers of neglecting it, and practical ways to develop this essential gift.

The Importance of Spiritual Discernment

Discernment is more than the ability to recognize right from wrong; it is the ability to distinguish God's truth from half-truths, counterfeits, and distractions. Scripture warns us repeatedly about deception. Jesus Himself said, "Beware of false prophets, who come to you in sheep's clothing but inwardly are ravenous wolves" (Matthew 7:15). In today's world, this deception can take many forms—cultural norms, social movements, and even organizations that appear good on the surface but are not rooted in God.

As Christians, we are called to test everything against the Word of God. This requires an intimate relationship with Scripture, consistent prayer, and reliance on the Holy Spirit. Without discernment, we risk being led astray by ideas, practices, or affiliations that pull us away from our identity in Christ.

The Dangers of Neglecting Discernment

Neglecting spiritual discernment often leads to compromise. When believers fail to examine the spiritual roots and implications of their choices, they open the door to confusion, deception, and even bondage.

One of the greatest dangers is the allure of "good" things that are not necessarily of God. Many organizations, like the Divine Nine, promote values such as community service, education, and leadership—things that seem positive and worthwhile. However, if their practices and foundations are not aligned with God's Word, they can become stumbling blocks. For example, participating in rituals or oaths that conflict with biblical principles may seem harmless at first but can create spiritual strongholds over time.

This lack of discernment often leads to spiritual stagnation. Believers may find themselves trapped in cycles of frustration, wondering why they feel distant from God or why their lives lack peace and purpose. The enemy thrives in these moments of spiritual blindness, using them to distract us from our God-given mission.

How to Develop Spiritual Discernment

1. Seek God Through His Word

The foundation of discernment is a deep understanding of Scripture. The Bible is our ultimate guide, providing wisdom, correction, and instruction for every area of life. Hebrews 4:12 reminds us, "For the word of God is alive and active. Sharper than any double-edged sword, it penetrates even to dividing soul and spirit, joints and marrow; it judges the thoughts and attitudes of the heart."

To develop discernment, commit to daily Bible study. Ask God to reveal His truth and expose anything in your life that does not align with His Word.

2. Pray for Wisdom

James 1:5 promises, "If any of you lacks wisdom, you should ask God, who gives generously to all without finding fault, and it will be given to you." Prayer is a powerful tool for discernment. Ask God for clarity, guidance, and the ability to see situations and decisions from His perspective.

Make prayer a dialogue, not just a monologue. Take time to listen to the Holy Spirit, who will prompt you, caution you, and affirm God's direction for your life.

3. Rely on the Holy Spirit

The Holy Spirit is our Helper and Teacher, guiding us into all truth (John 16:13). Cultivating a relationship with the Holy Spirit requires surrender, sensitivity, and obedience. When you sense a check in your spirit about a person, opportunity, or organization, take it seriously and seek confirmation from God.

Learn to recognize the peace of God as a marker of His approval. As Colossians 3:15 says, "Let the peace of Christ rule in your hearts."

4. Test Everything

First Thessalonians 5:21-22 instructs us to "test all things; hold fast what is good. Abstain from every form of evil." This means evaluating every decision, relationship, and commitment through the lens of Scripture.

Ask yourself:

- Does this align with God's Word?

- Does this bring glory to God?

- Does this draw me closer to God or pull me away?

- Would I feel comfortable explaining this decision to God Himself?

If the answer to any of these questions raises doubts, reconsider your choice.

5. Surround Yourself with Godly Counsel

Proverbs 11:14 reminds us, "Where there is no counsel, the people fall; but in the multitude of counselors, there is safety." Surround yourself with mature believers who can offer wisdom, accountability, and encouragement. They can help you discern God's will and avoid pitfalls.

6. Be Willing to Let Go

Developing discernment often means making difficult choices. When God reveals that something in your life is not of Him, you must be willing to let it go. This could mean walking away from relationships, habits, or affiliations that are not aligned with His will.

Letting go is not always easy, but it is necessary for spiritual growth. Trust that God has something better for you—something that will bring true peace, joy, and purpose.

Living a Life of Discernment

Discernment is not a one-time achievement; it is a daily practice. It requires vigilance, humility, and a willingness to submit every aspect of your life to God. As you grow in discernment, you will find greater freedom, clarity, and confidence in your walk with Christ.

A life of discernment honors God and protects you from the enemy's schemes. It allows you to fulfill your calling without distraction or compromise, ensuring that every decision you make is rooted in God's truth.

A Final Word of Encouragement

The call to spiritual discernment is a call to deeper intimacy with God. It is an invitation to trust Him fully, seek His wisdom, and walk in His ways. As you pursue discernment, remember that God is faithful to guide you. He will never leave you to navigate life's challenges alone.

Through prayer, Scripture, and the power of the Holy Spirit, you can develop the discernment needed to live a life that glorifies God and reflects His truth to the world. Stand firm in your faith, seek His will above all else, and let spiritual discernment be your guide.

Chapter 6:

What Does God Require of Us?

When we consider the question, "What does God require of us?" the answer is both profound and simple. God's requirements are not burdensome; they are rooted in His love for us and His desire for us to live in communion with Him. He created us for a purpose, and His Word provides clear guidance on how to fulfill that purpose. In this chapter, we will examine what God requires of us as individuals and as a community of believers, focusing on biblical principles that lead to a life of obedience, faithfulness, and spiritual fulfillment.

The Foundation of God's Requirements

Micah 6:8 provides a concise yet powerful summary of what God desires:

"He has shown you, O mortal, what is good.
And what does the Lord require of you?
To act justly and to love mercy
and to walk humbly with your God."

This verse captures the essence of God's will for our lives:

1. **Act Justly**: Live with integrity, fairness, and righteousness in all your dealings.

2. **Love Mercy**: Show compassion, forgiveness, and kindness to others.

3. **Walk Humbly**: Cultivate a close, dependent relationship with God, acknowledging His sovereignty and grace.

God's requirements are not about rigid rules or religious rituals. Instead, they call us to live in a way that reflects His character and brings glory to His name.

Living in Obedience to God

Obedience is central to our relationship with God. Jesus said, "If you love me, keep my commands" (John 14:15). Obedience is not about legalism but about love and trust. It is our response to God's grace and a demonstration of our faith in Him.

What Does Obedience Look Like?

1. **Surrendering Our Will**: Obedience begins with surrender. We must submit every area of our lives—our desires, plans, and decisions—to God. Romans 12:1-2 calls us to offer our bodies as living sacrifices and to be transformed by the renewing of our minds.

2. **Following God's Word**: The Bible is our ultimate authority. To obey God, we must know His Word and apply it to our lives. Psalm 119:105 says, "Your word is a lamp to my feet and a light to my path."

3. **Trusting His Plan**: Obedience often requires stepping out in faith, even when we don't fully understand God's plan. Proverbs 3:5-6 reminds us to trust in the Lord with all our hearts and to lean not on our own understanding.

Living in Holiness

God calls us to be holy because He is holy (1 Peter 1:16). Holiness is not about perfection; it is about being set apart for God's purposes. It involves turning away from sin and pursuing a life that reflects God's character.

How to Pursue Holiness

1. **Repentance**: Holiness begins with a heart of repentance. Acknowledge your sins, confess them to God, and turn away from them.

2. **Sanctification**: Allow the Holy Spirit to work in you, transforming you into the image of Christ. This is a lifelong process that requires patience and humility.

3. **Guarding Your Heart**: Be vigilant about what you allow into your mind and spirit. Proverbs 4:23 says, "Above all else, guard your heart, for everything you do flows from it."

Living in Love

God's greatest requirement is love. Jesus said, "Love the Lord your God with all your heart and with all your soul and with all your mind. This is the first and greatest commandment. And the second is like it: Love your neighbor as yourself" (Matthew 22:37-39).

What Does Love Look Like?

1. **Loving God**: Loving God means putting Him first in every aspect of your life. It means worshiping Him with your actions, words, and thoughts.

2. **Loving Others**: Loving others means showing kindness, compassion, and forgiveness, even to those who are difficult to love. It means putting their needs above your own and seeking their good.

Walking in Faithfulness

Faithfulness is about consistency and commitment. God requires us to remain steadfast in our relationship with Him, even in the face of trials and challenges.

How to Remain Faithful

1. **Daily Communion with God**: Spend time with God through prayer, worship, and Bible study. This strengthens your relationship with Him and keeps you grounded in His truth.

2. **Perseverance**: Faithfulness requires perseverance. Galatians 6:9 encourages us, "Let us not become weary in doing good, for at the proper time we will reap a harvest if we do not give up."

3. **Accountability**: Surround yourself with other believers who can encourage you, pray for you, and hold you accountable in your walk with God.

Impacting the World for God's Glory

God requires us not only to live for Him but also to impact the world around us. Matthew 5:16 says, "Let your light shine before others, that they may see your good deeds and glorify your Father in heaven."

Ways to Impact the World

1. **Sharing the Gospel**: Be bold in sharing the message of salvation with others. God calls us to be His ambassadors (2 Corinthians 5:20).

2. **Serving Others**: Use your gifts, talents, and resources to serve those in need. This reflects God's love and compassion.

3. **Being a Witness**: Live in a way that points others to Christ. Your actions, attitudes, and choices should reflect God's character and truth.

A Heart Fully Devoted to God

Ultimately, what God requires of us is a heart fully devoted to Him. He desires a relationship with us, not just religious observance. He wants us to trust Him, obey Him, and love Him with everything we have.

Deuteronomy 10:12-13 beautifully sums up what God asks of us:

"And now, Israel, what does the Lord your God ask of you but to fear the Lord your God, to walk in obedience to Him, to love Him, to serve the Lord your God with all your heart and with all your soul, and to observe the Lord's commands and decrees that I am giving you today for your own good?"

God's requirements are not burdensome; they are life-giving. As we align our lives with His will, we experience the fullness of His love, peace, and purpose.

Let this chapter serve as a reminder that God's call is not about perfection but about surrender and growth. He requires our trust, our obedience, and our devotion. As we answer His call, we discover the joy and freedom of walking in His ways.

Chapter 7:

Navigating Challenges and Making Informed Decisions

As Christians, we are called to live in the world but not be of the world (John 17:14-16). This call often requires discernment, especially when engaging with cultural, social, or organizational structures that may conflict with biblical principles. For Christians involved in, or considering joining, Divine Nine organizations, the challenge lies in navigating these affiliations in a way that honors God. In this chapter, we will outline practical steps for addressing these challenges, provide tools for discernment, and discuss how to remain rooted in one's faith.

1. Understanding Your Identity in Christ

Key Scripture:

• *"But you are a chosen people, a royal priesthood, a holy nation, God's special possession, that you may declare the praises of Him who called you out of darkness into His wonderful light."* (1 Peter 2:9)

The Foundation of Your Identity:
Christians must recognize that their primary identity is in Christ. This identity transcends earthly affiliations, titles, or memberships. Before committing to any organization, believers

must evaluate how the group aligns with or detracts from their identity as children of God.

Practical Steps:

1. **Reaffirm Your Identity Daily**: Spend time in prayer and Scripture, grounding yourself in who God says you are.

2. **Evaluate Competing Identities**: Consider whether membership in an organization might overshadow or conflict with your Christian identity.

3. **Be Honest About Motivations**: Reflect on why you are drawn to the organization. Is it for networking, status, or a sense of belonging? Ensure these desires align with biblical priorities.

2. Praying for Wisdom and Discernment

Key Scripture:

• *"If any of you lacks wisdom, you should ask God, who gives generously to all without finding fault, and it will be given to you."* (James 1:5)

The Role of Prayer:
Prayer is essential in seeking God's guidance about joining or remaining in any organization. Through prayer, Christians can ask for clarity, wisdom, and conviction.

Practical Steps:

1. **Ask for Guidance**: Pray specifically about your involvement in the organization, asking God to reveal His will.

2. **Seek Confirmation**: Look for confirmation through Scripture, godly counsel, and circumstances.

3. **Be Open to Conviction**: If God reveals areas of compromise or misalignment with His Word, be willing to adjust your decisions accordingly.

3. Seeking Counsel from Trusted Christian Leaders

Key Scripture:

- *"Plans fail for lack of counsel, but with many advisers, they succeed."* (Proverbs 15:22)

The Importance of Godly Counsel:
Trusted pastors, mentors, or Christian friends can provide insight and accountability as you evaluate your relationship with Divine Nine organizations.

Practical Steps:

1. **Choose Counselors Wisely**: Seek advice from mature believers who know you well and are grounded in Scripture.

2. **Be Transparent**: Share your concerns, motivations, and questions openly.

3. **Weigh Their Input**: Consider their perspectives prayerfully, but always align their advice with God's Word.

4. Evaluating Organizational Practices Through a Biblical Lens

Key Scripture:

- *"Test everything. Hold on to what is good, reject every kind of evil."* (1 Thessalonians 5:21-22)

Critical Evaluation:

Christians must examine the practices, rituals, and values of an organization to determine whether they align with biblical teachings.

Practical Steps:

1. **Research the Organization**: Understand its history, values, and practices.

2. **Compare Practices to Scripture**: Identify any elements that conflict with God's Word, such as idolatry, secrecy, or oaths.

3. **Consider Long-Term Impacts**: Reflect on how your involvement might influence your spiritual growth, witness, and priorities.

5. Establishing Boundaries

Key Scripture:

- *"Do not conform to the pattern of this world, but be transformed by the renewing of your mind."* (Romans 12:2)

Why Boundaries Are Necessary:

If you choose to remain in or join a Divine Nine organization, setting clear boundaries is critical to maintain your faith and witness.

Practical Steps:

1. **Define Non-Negotiables**: Identify specific practices or events you will not participate in if they conflict with your faith.

2. **Communicate Your Boundaries**: Be clear with fellow members about your convictions and limits.

3. **Stay Accountable**: Share your boundaries with a trusted Christian mentor who can support you in staying true to them.

6. Balancing Service with Spiritual Priorities

Key Scripture:

- *"Seek first His kingdom and His righteousness, and all these things will be given to you as well."* (Matthew 6:33)

Aligning Service with Faith:

Service is a core value of many Divine Nine organizations, but Christians must ensure that their service does not overshadow their spiritual responsibilities.

Practical Steps:

1. **Evaluate Your Motives**: Serve others out of love for God, not for recognition or obligation to the organization.

2. **Prioritize Church Involvement**: Make sure your service within the organization does not detract from your involvement in your local church or ministry.

3. **Share the Gospel**: Use your platform within the organization as an opportunity to point others to Christ.

7. Remaining a Light in the Organization

Key Scripture:

• *"You are the light of the world. A town built on a hill cannot be hidden."* (Matthew 5:14)

Living Out Your Faith:
If you choose to remain in a Divine Nine organization, you have the opportunity to be a light for Christ. This requires boldness, consistency, and humility.

Practical Steps:

1. **Live with Integrity**: Ensure that your actions, words, and attitudes reflect Christ.

2. **Be Open About Your Faith**: Share your testimony and convictions with others in the organization.

3. **Stand Firm Under Pressure**: Be prepared to face criticism or challenges for your faith, and respond with grace and truth.

8. Knowing When to Walk Away

Key Scripture:

• *"Therefore come out from them and be separate, says the Lord."* (2 Corinthians 6:17)

Discerning the Right Time:

If your involvement in a Divine Nine organization consistently leads to spiritual compromise or hinders your relationship with God, it may be time to leave.

Practical Steps:

1. **Seek God's Guidance**: Pray for clarity and peace about your decision.

2. **Consider Your Witness**: Reflect on whether your involvement is enhancing or detracting from your ability to share the gospel.

3. **Exit Gracefully**: If you choose to leave, do so with humility and respect, explaining your decision honestly.

Navigating the challenges of Divine Nine involvement requires wisdom, discernment, and a steadfast commitment to God's Word. By understanding your identity in Christ, seeking godly counsel, evaluating practices biblically, and setting clear boundaries, you can make informed decisions that honor your faith.

Whether you choose to remain in, join, or walk away from such organizations, remember that your ultimate allegiance is to Christ. The next chapter will explore how to maintain spiritual growth and integrity regardless of the outcome of your decision, ensuring that your faith remains the cornerstone of your life.

Chapter 8:

Maintaining Spiritual Growth and Integrity

The Christian life is a journey of continual growth in faith and character. Whether you choose to remain in, join, or separate from a Divine Nine organization, your spiritual growth and integrity must remain your highest priorities. This chapter provides practical steps for deepening your relationship with God, staying rooted in biblical truth, and guarding your witness in the world.

1. Staying Rooted in the Word of God

Key Scripture:

- *"Your word is a lamp to my feet and a light to my path."* (Psalm 119:105)

The Role of Scripture:
The Bible is the foundation for a Christian's faith and the ultimate guide for decision-making. Regular study of Scripture strengthens your understanding of God's will and equips you to discern truth from error.

Practical Steps:

1. **Daily Bible Reading**: Commit to reading and meditating on Scripture every day. Use a reading plan to stay consistent.

2. **Memorize Key Verses**: Equip yourself with Scriptures that address identity, discernment, and spiritual growth, such as Romans 12:2 and Matthew 6:33.

3. **Seek Biblical Wisdom**: Apply the principles of Scripture to all areas of your life, including your relationships and affiliations.

Reflection:

When faced with challenges or uncertainties, let God's Word guide your decisions and strengthen your convictions.

2. Cultivating a Life of Prayer

Key Scripture:

- *"Pray without ceasing."* (1 Thessalonians 5:17)

The Power of Prayer:

Prayer is essential for maintaining intimacy with God and seeking His guidance. Through prayer, you can bring your concerns, decisions, and challenges before Him, trusting in His wisdom and provision.

Practical Steps:

1. **Set a Prayer Schedule**: Dedicate specific times each day for focused prayer.

2. **Pray for Discernment**: Ask God for wisdom in navigating organizational involvement and other life decisions.

3. **Intercede for Others**: Pray for fellow believers, your church, and even members of your organization, asking God to work in their lives.

Reflection:

Prayer is not just a duty but a privilege that connects you to the Creator. Make it the cornerstone of your spiritual life.

3. Remaining Active in Christian Community

Key Scripture:

- *"And let us consider how we may spur one another on toward love and good deeds, not giving up meeting together, as some are in the habit of doing, but encouraging one another."* (Hebrews 10:24-25)

The Importance of Fellowship:

Participation in a local church and Christian community is vital for spiritual growth. Fellow believers provide encouragement, accountability, and support as you navigate life's challenges.

Practical Steps:

1. **Commit to a Local Church**: Be actively involved in a Bible-believing church that encourages spiritual growth.

2. **Join a Small Group**: Participate in Bible studies or discipleship groups to deepen your understanding of God's Word.

3. **Be Accountable**: Share your challenges and decisions with trusted Christian friends or mentors who can guide and pray for you.

Reflection:

Isolation can lead to spiritual stagnation. Stay connected to a community that challenges you to grow in faith and love.

4. Practicing Integrity in All Areas of Life

Key Scripture:

- *"Whatever you do, work at it with all your heart, as working for the Lord, not for human masters."* (Colossians 3:23)

Living a Life of Integrity:

Integrity means aligning your actions, words, and decisions with biblical principles. This is especially important when navigating environments where your faith may be tested.

Practical Steps:

1. **Be Consistent**: Ensure that your private life reflects the same faith and values you display publicly.

2. **Stand Firm in Convictions**: Do not compromise your beliefs, even when faced with peer pressure or criticism.

3. **Represent Christ Well**: In all your interactions, strive to be a reflection of God's love, grace, and truth.

Reflection:

Integrity is a powerful testimony to the transformative work of Christ in your life. Let your character and actions point others to Him.

5. Guarding Your Heart and Mind

Key Scripture:

- *"Above all else, guard your heart, for everything you do flows from it."* (Proverbs 4:23)

Protecting Your Inner Life:
The world is filled with influences that can distract or mislead believers. Guarding your heart and mind involves being intentional about what you consume and how you respond to challenges.

Practical Steps:

1. **Filter Your Influences**: Be mindful of the media, conversations, and activities you engage in, ensuring they align with your faith.

2. **Renew Your Mind**: Regularly renew your thoughts through Scripture and prayer, as Romans 12:2 instructs.

3. **Stay Focused on God's Purpose**: Avoid distractions that pull you away from your spiritual priorities and calling.

Reflection:
What you allow into your heart and mind shapes your spiritual health. Be diligent in protecting them from harmful influences.

6. Witnessing to Others Through Your Faith

Key Scripture:

- *"In the same way, let your light shine before others, that they may see your good deeds and glorify your Father in heaven."* (Matthew 5:16)

Being a Light in the World:
Your life is a testimony to God's work. Whether you are engaging with members of a Divine Nine organization or others in your community, your actions and words should reflect Christ's love and truth.

Practical Steps:

1. **Share the Gospel Boldly**: Look for opportunities to share your faith with others, especially those who may not know Christ.

2. **Live a Life of Love**: Demonstrate the fruit of the Spirit—love, joy, peace, patience, kindness, goodness, faithfulness, gentleness, and self-control (Galatians 5:22-23).

3. **Be Prepared to Answer**: Study Scripture so you can confidently respond to questions about your faith (1 Peter 3:15).

Reflection:
Your witness is one of the most powerful ways to glorify God and draw others to Him. Let your life be a beacon of hope and truth.

7. Trusting God with the Outcome

Key Scripture:

• *"Trust in the Lord with all your heart and lean not on your own understanding; in all your ways submit to Him, and He will make your paths straight."* (Proverbs 3:5-6)

Relying on God's Sovereignty:
As you navigate decisions and challenges, trust that God is in control. He is faithful to guide, provide, and sustain you as you seek to honor Him.

Practical Steps:

1. **Surrender Your Plans**: Submit your decisions and goals to God, trusting His wisdom over your own.

2. **Walk in Faith**: Even when the path is unclear, trust that God will direct your steps.

3. **Rest in His Promises**: Remember that God is with you and will never leave or forsake you (Deuteronomy 31:6).

Reflection:
Spiritual growth requires dependence on God. Trust Him to lead you and work all things for your good and His glory (Romans 8:28).

Spiritual growth and integrity are lifelong pursuits that require intentionality, discipline, and faith. By staying rooted in Scripture, cultivating a life of prayer, engaging with a Christian community, and living with integrity, you can honor God in all areas of your life.

Whether your journey involves remaining in a Divine Nine organization, stepping away, or taking another path, your ultimate priority is to glorify God and grow in your relationship with Him. As we transition to the final chapter, we will explore how to inspire and guide others who face similar challenges, encouraging them to remain steadfast in their faith.

Chapter 9:

Inspiring Others to Remain Steadfast in Faith

Christianity is not just a personal journey but a collective mission. As believers, we are called to encourage and strengthen one another in faith, especially those facing challenges in navigating cultural and organizational affiliations. This chapter focuses on how you can inspire others to remain steadfast in their commitment to Christ, providing guidance, encouragement, and a godly example.

1. Embracing the Role of a Spiritual Mentor

Key Scripture:

- *"Follow my example, as I follow the example of Christ."* (1 Corinthians 11:1)

The Power of Mentorship:
Mentorship is a biblical principle. Paul mentored Timothy, Naomi guided Ruth, and Jesus mentored His disciples. As you grow in your faith, you have the opportunity to disciple others, helping them navigate their own spiritual journeys.

Practical Steps:

1. **Be an Example**: Live out your faith in a way that others can imitate. Your life should reflect integrity, humility, and love.

2. **Offer Guidance**: Share your experiences, insights, and the lessons God has taught you, particularly in areas like navigating organizational affiliations.

3. **Invest in Relationships**: Build authentic connections with those you mentor, making time to listen, pray, and support them.

Reflection:
Discipleship is not about perfection but about pointing others to Christ through your words and actions.

2. Encouraging Others to Seek God's Word

Key Scripture:

• *"Let the message of Christ dwell among you richly as you teach and admonish one another with all wisdom."* (Colossians 3:16)

Why Scripture is Essential:
The Bible is the ultimate source of truth and guidance. Encouraging others to prioritize Scripture equips them to discern truth, combat spiritual deception, and grow in their relationship with God.

Practical Steps:

1. **Study Scripture Together**: Organize Bible studies or small groups where you can explore God's Word with others.

2. **Provide Resources**: Share books, devotionals, or study guides that focus on spiritual growth and discernment.

3. **Teach Biblical Principles**: Help others apply Scripture to real-life situations, particularly when facing conflicts between cultural norms and biblical teachings.

Reflection:
When you guide others to rely on God's Word, you empower them to stand firm in their faith.

3. Offering Encouragement in the Face of Challenges

Key Scripture:

- *"Therefore encourage one another and build each other up, just as in fact you are doing."* (1 Thessalonians 5:11)

The Need for Encouragement:
Navigating spiritual conflicts can be isolating and discouraging. By offering encouragement, you can remind others that they are not alone and that God is faithful to strengthen and sustain them.

Practical Steps:

1. **Be a Listening Ear**: Let others share their struggles without fear of judgment.

2. **Remind Them of God's Promises**: Share Scriptures that emphasize God's faithfulness, such as Isaiah 41:10 and Philippians 4:13.

3. **Celebrate Spiritual Victories**: Acknowledge and celebrate steps of faith, no matter how small, as they seek to honor God.

Reflection:
A simple word of encouragement can renew someone's faith and resolve to follow Christ.

4. Helping Others Navigate Organizational Challenges

Key Scripture:

- *"Carry each other's burdens, and in this way, you will fulfill the law of Christ."* (Galatians 6:2)

Providing Practical Support:
For Christians struggling with their involvement in Divine Nine organizations, practical guidance and spiritual support are crucial.

Practical Steps:

1. **Guide Them in Prayer**: Encourage them to seek God's direction and provide opportunities to pray with them.

2. **Share Biblical Insights**: Help them evaluate the organization's practices through a biblical lens.

3. **Respect Their Journey**: Understand that everyone's spiritual walk is different and allow them the space to make decisions while supporting them in love.

Reflection:
Your role is not to impose decisions but to provide support, wisdom, and encouragement as they seek God's will.

5. Fostering a Culture of Accountability

Key Scripture:

- *"As iron sharpens iron, so one person sharpens another."* (Proverbs 27:17)

Why Accountability Matters:
Accountability helps believers stay on track in their spiritual journey. It creates a safe space for growth, confession, and encouragement.

Practical Steps:

1. **Create Accountability Groups**: Encourage regular check-ins with a small group of believers.

2. **Be Honest and Transparent**: Model vulnerability by sharing your own challenges and victories.

3. **Encourage Confession and Prayer**: Remind others of the power of confessing struggles and seeking God's forgiveness (James 5:16).

Reflection:
Accountability is a gift that helps Christians stay grounded and supported in their faith.

6. Inspiring Others Through Your Testimony

Key Scripture:

- *"They triumphed over him by the blood of the Lamb and by the word of their testimony."* (Revelation 12:11)

The Impact of Testimonies:
Your personal story of faith, struggles, and victories can inspire others to remain steadfast. It reminds them of God's power and faithfulness.

Practical Steps:

1. **Share Your Story Boldly**: Be willing to share how God has worked in your life, including your experiences with organizational involvement.

2. **Highlight God's Faithfulness**: Focus on how God's grace and guidance have sustained you.

3. **Invite Others to Reflect**: Encourage others to see how God is working in their own lives.

Reflection:
A testimony is not just a recounting of events but a declaration of God's glory and power.

7. Trusting God to Work in Their Lives

Key Scripture:

• *"Being confident of this, that He who began a good work in you will carry it on to completion until the day of Christ Jesus."* (Philippians 1:6)

Relying on God's Sovereignty:
Ultimately, spiritual growth is God's work. While you can plant seeds and water them, it is God who brings the increase (1 Corinthians 3:6-7). Trust Him to guide others according to His will.

Practical Steps:

1. **Pray for Their Growth**: Commit to regularly praying for those you are mentoring or supporting.

2. **Release Control**: Recognize that their journey is between them and God.

3. **Celebrate God's Work**: Rejoice in the progress and transformation God brings about in their lives.

Reflection:

Your role is to encourage and inspire, trusting God to do the transformative work in their hearts.

Inspiring others to remain steadfast in faith is a high calling and a profound privilege. By mentoring, encouraging, and sharing your testimony, you can help others navigate challenges while pointing them to Christ.

As you seek to inspire others, remember that your ultimate goal is not to win debates or enforce decisions but to lead them closer to God. Trust that the Holy Spirit will work in their hearts and guide them in truth.

The journey of faith is not meant to be traveled alone. By supporting one another in love and truth, we reflect the unity and strength of the body of Christ, bringing glory to God and expanding His kingdom on earth.

Conclusion:

A Call to Faithful Discipleship and Bold Obedience

As we come to the end of this exploration, it is clear that the journey of faith is one that requires unwavering commitment, discernment, and integrity. The issues raised in this book are not easy, nor are they without personal and communal challenges. The Divine Nine organizations, like many cultural constructs, often present tension for believers who desire to live according to the teachings of Scripture. While these organizations may offer a sense of community, identity, and belonging, it is essential to evaluate their practices and values through the lens of God's Word.

Throughout the chapters, we have examined how certain practices within the Divine Nine organizations conflict with biblical principles and what it means to remain faithful to Christ despite cultural and social pressures. The Bible calls us to be "in the world but not of the world" (John 17:14-16), to be salt and light (Matthew 5:13-16), and to pursue holiness in all areas of life. Our ultimate allegiance is to Christ alone, and no affiliation—whether social, political, or organizational—should compromise our primary identity as children of God.

However, this book has not only highlighted the dangers of compromise but also emphasized the call to spiritual growth and integrity. Maintaining a vibrant relationship with God, staying rooted in Scripture, and pursuing a life of prayer, accountability, and witness are essential to remaining steadfast in the faith. As believers, we must be diligent in protecting our hearts and minds from the influence of secular ideologies and false teachings. We are called to pursue righteousness, honor God in all things, and be an example to others in our community.

Yet, the journey of faith is not a solitary one. As we walk out our own convictions, we are tasked with helping others do the same. We are called to encourage, mentor, and inspire fellow believers who may be struggling with the same questions, decisions, and cultural pressures. Through the power of testimony, prayer, and accountability, we can help others navigate the challenges of their faith journeys, urging them to remain faithful to the gospel and the truth of God's Word.

Ultimately, this is a call to faithful discipleship and bold obedience to Christ. It is a call to live with courage in a world that often asks us to compromise our beliefs. It is a call to prioritize Christ above all else—above societal expectations, organizational allegiances, and personal desires. In doing so, we not only honor God but also fulfill our highest calling as His ambassadors on earth.

As you reflect on the content of this book, I encourage you to take a personal inventory of your own life and affiliations. Ask yourself where your true allegiance lies. Is it with Christ, or are there areas where the influence of cultural, social, or organizational pressures has caused you to compromise? Seek God's guidance, listen to the Holy Spirit, and take bold steps toward living a life of full surrender to Him.

The journey of faith is not always easy, but it is worth it. Christ has called us to follow Him, and as we do so, we can trust that He will provide the strength, wisdom, and grace we need. Stand firm in your faith, be a light to others, and live out the truth of God's Word in every aspect of your life.

May you continue to grow in the knowledge and grace of our Lord Jesus Christ, and may your life bring glory to God in all that you do.

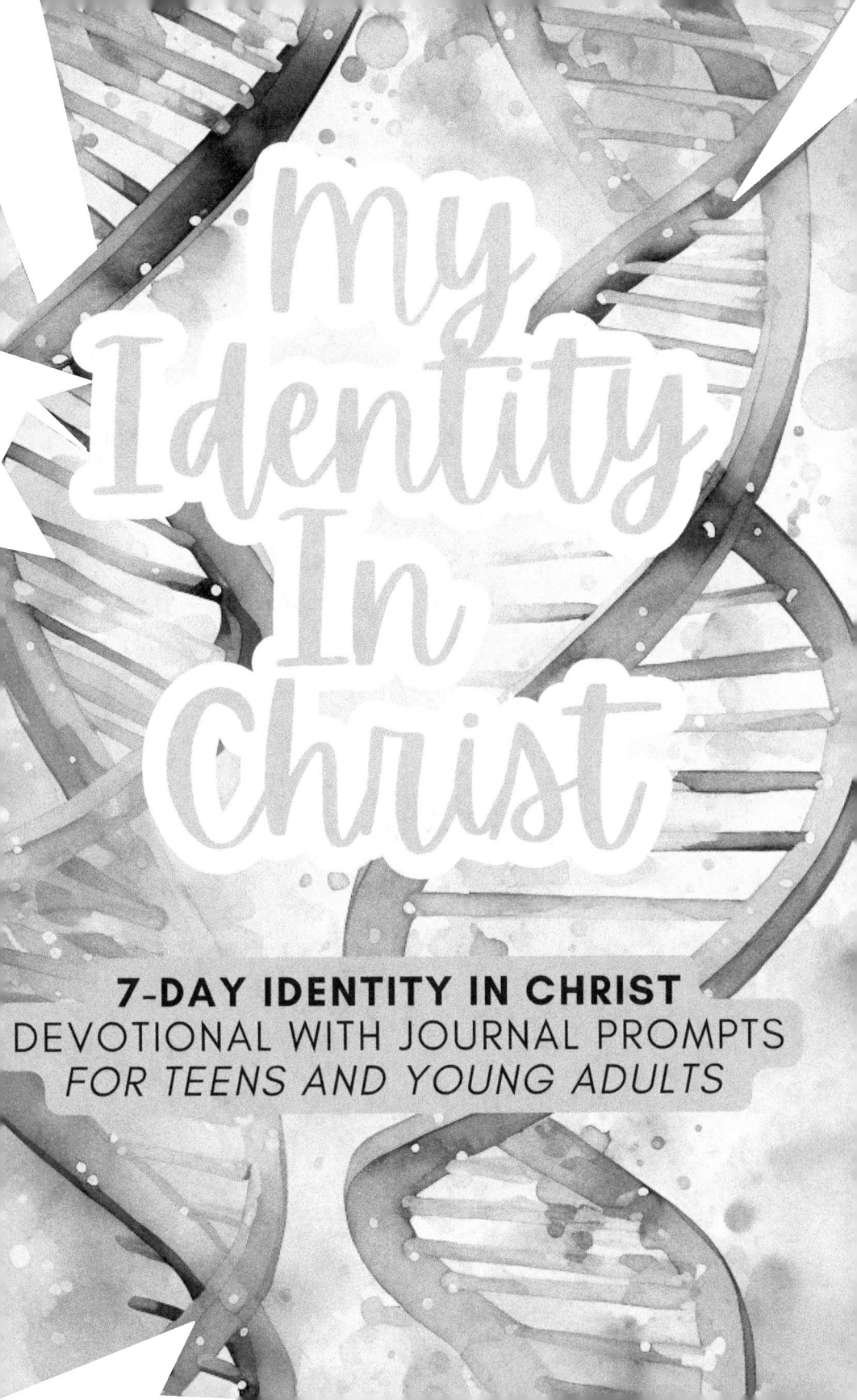

The teen and young adult years can be very confusing. We live in a world that is always trying to create our identities and pull us away from our Creator, God. Amidst the noise and chaos of societal pressures and cultural expectations, it's easy to lose sight of who we truly are and whose we are.

This 7-day mini-devotional serves as a reminder of who God says you are and that your identity is found in Him alone. Go through each day and ask God to help you perceive the love He has for you and what it really means to have your identity in Him.

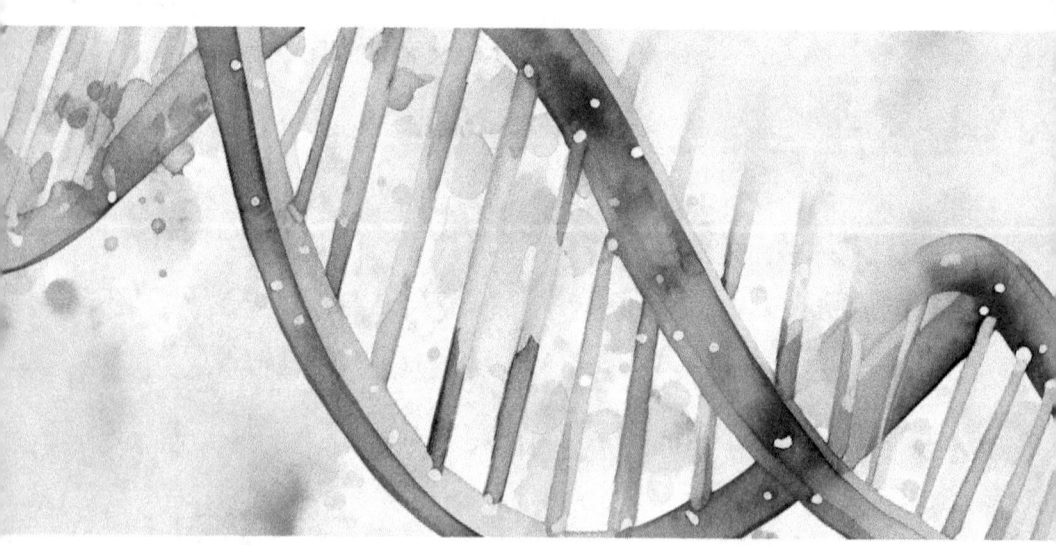

Day 1: Knowing Who You Are in Christ
Ephesians 2:10 For we are his workmanship, created in Christ Jesus for good works, which God prepared beforehand, that we should walk in them.

Understanding that you are God's masterpiece created in Christ Jesus is foundational to your identity. Let's take a closer look at this verse.

"For we are his workmanship": This phrase emphasizes that believers are God's creation. The word "workmanship" comes from the Greek word "poiéma," which means "a product". This highlights the idea that each believer is uniquely crafted by God with care and intentionality.

"Created in Christ Jesus": This phrase indicates that our identity as God's workmanship is found in our relationship with Christ. It emphasizes that our spiritual rebirth and transformation occur through our union with Christ. Our new identity and purpose stems from being "in Christ Jesus."

"For good works": This clause highlights the purpose for which we are created. Believers are not only saved by grace but also called to a life of good works. These good works are the natural outflow of our faith in Christ and are intended to bring glory to God and benefit others.

"Which God prepared beforehand": This phrase emphasizes that God has already planned and prepared specific good works for each believer to walk in.

"That we should walk in them": This clause stresses the importance of actively living out the good works that God has prepared for us. It implies a lifestyle characterized by obedience to God's will and a willingness to engage in acts of service and love towards others. But it also implies that we have free will and can choose to be obedient or not.

Journal Prompt: Reflect on a time when you felt uncertain about your identity. How does knowing that you are God's masterpiece, handiwork, or workmanship created in Christ Jesus change your perspective on your worth and purpose?

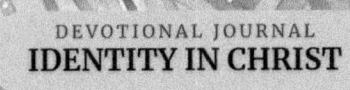

Day 2: Identity Secure in Christ

1 John 1a See what great love the Father has lavished on us, that we should be called children of God! And that is what we are!

The apostle John reminds us of the incredible love that God has poured out upon us. It is a love that transcends human understanding, a love that declares us as beloved children of the Most High. Our identity as children of God is not based on our performance or circumstances, but on the unchanging character of our Heavenly Father. In Christ, we find our security. We are chosen, accepted, and cherished by God Himself. Our worth is not determined by the fleeting opinions of others, but by the priceless sacrifice of Jesus on the cross. Through His death and resurrection, we are made new, clothed in His righteousness, and invited into a relationship of intimacy and grace. As we anchor our identity in Christ, we can rest in the assurance of our salvation. We no longer need to strive for acceptance or approval from the world, for we are already fully accepted and deeply loved by our Heavenly Father.

Journal Prompt: Reflect on your understanding of identity. How have you defined yourself in the past? How does knowing that you are secure in Christ as a beloved child of God impact the way you view yourself? How does this truth shape your sense of worth and purpose?

Day 3: Chosen and Called

1 Peter 2:9 But you are a chosen people, a royal priesthood, a holy nation, God's special possession, that you may declare the praises of him who called you out of darkness into his wonderful light.

God has chosen you and called you His own. God, who created all things, is your Father because of the faith you have in Jesus Christ. Isn't that amazing. Think about what it means to be chosen by God – that you are His kid – and how this impacts your purpose and direction in life.

Journal Prompt: Consider a time when you faced doubt or uncertainty about your purpose in life. How does knowing that you are chosen and called by God impact your confidence and sense of direction? Reflect on how embracing your identity as chosen and called by God empowers you to pursue your passions and serve others with purpose and conviction.

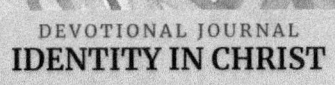
Day 4: Freedom in Christ

Galatians 5:1 It is for freedom that Christ has set us free. Stand firm, then, and do not let yourselves be burdened again by a yoke of slavery.

Christ has set you free from the bondage of sin and shame. Jesus Christ took your place in death. He died for you so that you would be free. Reflect on the freedom you have in Christ and how it empowers you to live a life of purpose and joy.

Journal Prompt: Reflect on a time when you experienced freedom from something. How does knowing that Christ has set you free and liberated you empower you to live a life of purpose and joy?

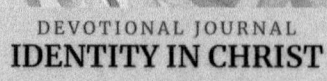

Day 5: Living in Victory

1 Corinthians 15:57 But thanks be to God! He gives us the victory through our Lord Jesus Christ.

Through Christ, you have victory over sin and death. 1 John 1:9 says If we confess our sins, he is faithful and just and will forgive us our sins and purify us from all unrighteousness. When you sin you can go to Jesus Christ and ask for forgiveness. He is faithful and just to forgive you of your sins. You do not have bear the shame of sinning against God. And you don't have to condemn yourself. Isn't that awesome??

Journal Prompt: Write about a recent victory or moment of triumph in your walk with Christ. How does knowing that you have victory through Christ no matter what happens impact your outlook on life and your future?

Day 6: Walking in His Image

Colossians 3:10 and have put on the new self, which is being renewed in knowledge in the image of its Creator.

As you grow in your relationship with Christ, you are being renewed in His image. Reflect on how you can reflect Christ's character more fully in your thoughts, words, and actions.

Journal Prompt: Identify a specific character trait of Christ (e.g., love, kindness, patience) that you want to cultivate in your own life. Reflect on ways you can actively reflect that trait in your thoughts, words, and actions.

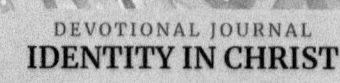
Day 7: The Love of God

Romans 8:38-39 For I am convinced that neither death nor life, neither angels nor demons, either the present nor the future, nor any powers, neither height nor depth, nor anything else in all creation, will be able to separate us from the love of God that is in Christ Jesus our Lord.

In these verses, the Apostle Paul declares the overwhelming certainty that nothing in all of creation can separate believers from the unwavering and boundless love of God, which is found in Christ Jesus our Lord. God's love for you is unchanging. Take time today to meditate on the depth of His love and how it impacts your sense of worth and belonging.

Journal Prompt: Search the Bible for more information on the love of God. How do you think Paul became convinced of this? How can you become more convinced of this?

www.ingramcontent.com/pod-product-compliance
Lightning Source LLC
Chambersburg PA
CBHW071115120626
46546CB00003B/1351